T0193839

Chapter 1

What Does The Word Say?

King David was on point when he penned Psalm 51:5. Yes. We were all born in sin and shapen in iniquity, but zealous religious leaders, parents, and grandparents have distorted the purity of this scripture, giving it an evil connotation by labeling sex as sinful. The scripture does not say, "We were born BY sin." We find this "tampering" put into practice often. Men and women of influence, in leadership positions, have misappropriated the Word of God.

In the book of Hebrews we learn that the marriage bed is honorable (3:4). Sex is a God-given gift allowing us to share in God's creative ability through procreation. Sex is a source of marital pleasure to be enjoyed within the bounds of what we now recognize as Holy Matrimony. (Genesis 2:24-25, Ephesians 5:25-29).

Many times, in our desperation to make citizens of The Kingdom walk in obedience, we try adding cultural flavor to strengthen the impact on the hearer of The Word. We are tempted to lean to our finite understanding.

We often create spiritual error, called *"bliptures," scriptures having no validation within the bible,* which when repeated, often become accepted as Truth. Such tactics never work, but tend to cloud the truth. These *bliptures* are likely to create mistrust, as well as confusion, within The Body of Christ. Such practices weaken our spiritual foundational structure as does untempered bricks which haven't been tried by fire (Ezekiel 12:13).

We must be mindful to never apply The Word deceitfully (2 Corinthians 4:2). By all means, with every opportunity, share The Word, but avoid sending mixed messages. There is never a reason to add to or take away from The Word.

This book is the author's attempt to try to address this type of error. May this awareness serve as a reminder to those aspiring to teach the truth of God's Word (James 3:1-12), to always be mindful of the biblical responsibility of a Teacher; which is a part *of the fivefold ministry gifts* (Ephesians 4:11-18).

The following *blipture*, which is often preached, taught, and even sung, is a perfect example:

"The race is not given to the swift, nor to the strong, but to him that endureth to the end."

This is not a scripture found anywhere in the Word of God, but is contrary to several truths verified within The Word (see Ecclesiastes 11:9-11a, Matthew 24:13). It sounds good, even makes a great song; but it contradicts Joshua 1:8, Deuteronomy 31:6, and Ephesians 6:10.

Maintaining erroneous doctrine in The Body of Christ is as lethal as hosting a deadly virus within the natural body. Each of us, negatively or positively, affects other members of the body. (Ephesians 4: 15-16, MSG).

Part of the problem is due to the lack of personal study of The Word of God. Today's society has encouraged a microwave mentality which says, "I want all my needs met void of any personal responsibility or effort on my part. I want it done my way, and I want it done yesterday." Everyone is in a hurry. We are seldom taught the true value of patience, a Fruit of The Holy Spirit (Galatians 5:22-23).

For example, if you choose to ignore the opening Disclaimer, along with the preface, and are now scanning through this introduction to try to determine whether or not to risk *wasting time*; or, you are knit-picking to find a reason to discontinue reading, you might be the classic example as to why we are not as well informed as we should be.

In baseball, for example, rushing to home plate without having tagged first base, we will discover the umpire at home plate, having the final say by displaying a hefty backward thumb!

All the speeding around the bases, the final long slide, bruised elbows, stressed muscles, and dirt in the face was for naught! You're OUT!

Or...

In football, you intercept a long pass, avoiding all attempts at blocking your sixty-five-yard return. You cross the goal line, lifting your arms, anticipating *"the thrill of victory"* only to discover *"the agony of defeat"* as you realize... there is a flag on the play.

You might be annoyed to find that there are no reference scriptures at the end of each paragraph, thus causing you to search. News flash! This project is designed to create the need to do just that; *search the scriptures* (John 5:39-47).

Discipline, as well as attention to every bit of content and context, is crucial as we walk this straight and narrow road to Eternal Life. Only through intentional intimacy with The Word of God and The God of The Word, will you be able to develop a fervent love for The Father (Matthew 11:18-30).

Everything you need to know is woven within the pages of this textbook called The Bible. All you have to do is prayerfully search (2 Timothy 2:15). Your one sure advantage is having the Master Teacher, the Holy Spirit, available *24/7/365*. Private tutoring is at your fingertips whether you are at home or away. The Holy Spirit will give you personal illumination and understanding.

God knows with whom He can trust His mysteries. He is only confident in those proven to be obedient, effective, and have a steadfast love for God and His people.

Loyalty and obedience are key ingredients to receiving the abundant favor of God (1 Corinthians 15:58). He is the same today, yesterday, and forever. He loves us all equally, but He pours out abundant favor as well as promotion to those who love Him most (John 21:17).

Chapter 2

A Divine Calling

My desire to share with believers and nonbelievers began years before becoming a Licensed or Ordained Minister in a local Baptist Denominational Church.

Totally inexperienced concerning the things of Christ, I had no idea that the increasing desire to talk about Jesus was evidence of the spiritual gift being birthed in me. This growing passion was a call within to teach (Ephesians 4:11).

While reading the Bible during breaks at a well-known bakery where I was employed, there was an urge to share "The Word" with my coworkers. I wanted everyone to know what I had discovered. My compassion pulsated for those who did not know how much God loves them.

Everything, people, places and things, looked and felt so different. Especially, my attitude was not the same. It wasn't that I was a difficult person to get along with, but there were times when I spoke without thinking. If asked to work overtime, I would give a lot of reasons and excuses. For example, "The supervisor didn't ask in time" or I would pretend to have an imaginary doctor's appointment. I had no problem refusing to cooperate. Refusing gave me a feeling of power.

Now, things were quite different! I became more willing to go the extra mile. My tolerance level changed. I became more sociable. I encouraged those in my department by singing and laughing while packing the donuts. We held hands and prayed before beginning our shift. *It was amazing!*

No one knows better than I, my continual need to grow, even after three decades of studying The Word. There is so much I need to learn. I suspect there are even some things I need to unlearn.

My beloved pastor helped me understand the changes I was experiencing. He was one of my prominent examples.

He never claimed to be perfect. The pastor led by example with a humble spirit. He was very fervent about The Word of God. He preached with The Fire of The Holy Ghost, always encouraging the congregation to develop a personal relationship with God through The Word.

He admonished us to always engage our bibles, carefully examining the text within every sermon. We were never to take anyone's word in place of God's Word. His handling of the scriptures was thorough, yet so simplistic that a child could understand. He often shared deep revelations with us, but there was always something for "babes" as well as for "meat-eaters" in the house (1st Corinthians 3:2).

Having no degrees of which to boast at that time, his fervent love for God, God's Word, and for the people of God, was apparent as well as very impressive. While under his pastoral influence I developed a love for The Word of God, following him as he followed Christ. I became anchored upon a solid foundation in Christ through the teaching of the uncompromised Gospel of Jesus Christ. The pastor had certain *"tags"* he used. Whether or not they were original I never knew. For example, he would say, while finding relevant scriptures:

"Let The Word do the talking."

When warning against erroneous preaching, he would say:

"Eat the meat and throw the bones away."

When admonishing about sharing The Gospel:

"Get all you can, can all you get, but don't sit on the can."

Until this day, there are other memorable *"grab and go nuggets"* stored in my memory. Sometimes I use them to discipline myself, for example, *no bible no breakfast, a reminder of the importance of spiritual food.*

Discipline in The Word helps you stand firm while growing in your personal Christian Experience. God's Word remains The Solid Rock. It never changes. The songwriter, Edward Motie, composer of the worthy hymn, Solid Rock, boldly acknowledged The Word of God as the only sure foundation for a life steadfast and sure.

This first church experience was later intensified in the fellowship I connected with after moving South. There, I found a rich and pure teaching that added to my already established faith in Christ. Oh what a fellowship I found waiting for me there. Living up to its name, Love and Faith Christian Fellowship, I was surprised to learn my new church home boast in Christ as being like The Philippian Church, having outpouring love for God, Love for the sinner, yet hating the sin. Philippians had long been one of my favorite books in the Bible.

Chapter 3

—◆—

Let's Grow Together

Having come from various persuasions, ethnicities, countries perhaps different ideologies.

those of you reading this book, have many differences. I realize we are not all believers however, hopefully we will form a bond which transcends all differences.

Those of us who have a relationship with God realize God's ways are not our ways and His thoughts are higher than ours (Isaiah 55:8-9). His wisdom is past finding out (Job 38 - 40). We are not trying to change God into our image and our likeness. On the contrary; we desire to become transformed (Romans:12:1-3). For those non believers, or skeptics, I ask that you be willing to put aside your old way of thinking and experience a new mindset for a brief time. We present to you the mind of Christ (Philippians 2:5).

At times we might find ourselves in rather awkward positions. This shifting of mindset does not always feel comfortable. We might want to revert to what comes easy or to the way we are used to doing things; for example, *the way our ancestors did it or* how *we were brought up.*

As believers, we've come to understand mankind is divided into two categories, believers, and non-believers. We all fit into one of these categories no matter your origin, ethnicity, nationality, or socioeconomic status. If you are a believer, you too might experience a change in belief or mindset, as well as a desire to change long practiced traditions. You must persevere, realizing this newness is a part of our growth process, developing from babes to effective servants of God.

The nonbelievers are free to leave this experience unimpacted. It's your choice. After all is said and done, it's your free will to decide. It is our prayer; however, that you will embrace The Faith we, as believers, have come to know and love.

As we mature in the things of God, we must always maintain a teachable attitude which is subject to be corrected by the Word of God. We must never become so familiar with the Word of God that we lose touch with The God of The Word. We should never think it is no longer necessary to prayerfully search the scriptures. We are to be reminded that we see through a glass darkly. We must always be receptive to correction that agrees with God's Word.

We are always students. There is never a time we stop learning because we feel as though we know it all. We should never be found using phrases such as, *"I've read that already, I know it by heart,* or *everybody knows that."* The more we know the more we realize we don't know all there is to know.

We should endeavor to become as young Jesus, who was found sitting among the Elders, learned men of that day, showing themselves approved by answering, posing questions and sharing answers. The young Jesus seated in their midst, was about His Father's business (Luke 2:42-49). They marveled at His wisdom. You too must ask questions, seek answers, but never for the purpose of debate. Be willing to share humbly what you receive, increasing in knowledge, strengthening and being strengthened, Iron sharpening Iron (Proverbs 27:17). Never be afraid to confess: *I don't know,* or to admit *you stand corrected.*

Within every fellowship, there are believers on different spiritual levels. There are babes who are growing on *The Sincere Milk.* You will find those mature believers, dining on the "meat" of The Word. They are the *Eagles who have learned to soar and are willing and able to help others take their first flight.* We want to associate ourselves with *Eagles* so that we too will learn to soar.

Within the body of christ are those referred to as "carnal minded" (1 Corinthians 3: 1-3). These believers, although saved, in comparison to the eagle, spend little time in The Word, in prayer and fellowship. They seem unconcerned about their level of spirituality. They have no interest in soaring but are content with their position on ground level. Spending quality time with *Turkeys* and remaining grounded will never inspire you to attempt your solo flight (Isaiah 40::31).

Successful eagles go through a yearly mulching process, ridding their bodies of old feathers which no longer serve effectively, thus allowing room for new growth. Some time transitioning can be painful. Always remember we are going through a continual process.

This is most effective when humbling oneself before God through regular self-examination of our intentions and motives (James 1:22-25, Hebrews 4:12). Never become so self-confident in your present position, but be ready to excel to what you are to become according to God's predestined plan for your life (Jeremiah 29:11-13). Humility is key to being used by God and growing in the things of God. Jesus is our greatest example of humility (Philippians2:6-8). God resists the proud but gives grace to the humble (James 4:6).

We pray to become mentors ourselves, helping to nourish God's lambs and sheep (John 21:17, Hebrews 5:12-14, KJV). May we be transformed from babes to mature servants who rightly divide The Word Of Truth.

It is my fervent prayer that we gain the support of those more learned, my spiritual brothers and sisters provoking the body unto good works. Consider this an official invitation to join us in this newfound fellowship. We need each other.

Some of us may be in fervent pursuit of high levels of academia or an entrepreneurial trailblazer, possessing strong leadership skills yet to be uncovered. You may be blessed to have enormous responsibilities while navigating a family through these present turbulent waters. Whatever your station in life, while studying and saturating your mind with God's Word, you will find your unique position, sharing gifts and callings within The Kingdom Fellowship. Perhaps you have already yielded to the innate calling on your life. You might have to make major shifts to move into your calling or gift, always mindful that His ways are not our ways. Don't close yourself or allow anyone to lock you in a box; thereby, depleting your God-given authority to operate within your gift. You can do all things and nothing is impossible for you. We can do it better if we do it together (Ephesians 4:11-16).

One thing must remain uppermost in our mind (John 15:1-5). We as Kingdom seekers, must cling to our Source rather than relying on our resources by remembering that true wisdom begins with a reverential fear of God. He is our true source (James 3:17). Any rebellion against The Will, Word, or Spirit of God is an exercise in total futility and vanity (1 Samuel 15:23). The scripture refers to it as *VAINGLORY* (*Galatians 5:26*).

Chapter 4

◆◆◆◆◆

We Must Agree

I pray the Holy Spirit plows up the fallow ground within us so we might sow, together, into good soil, (Matthew 13:3-9) allowing us to bring forth fruit of 30, 60 or even 100 fold.

A brief prayer:

Open our eyes, Lord, that we might see, our ears that we might hear, and our hearts, that we might receive from You today, Father, for Your Glory and our good. Amen.

The prophet Amos cautions that two cannot walk together except they be agreed (Amos 3:3). If we are members of the body of Christ, Jesus is your savior as He is mine; therefore, we walk in agreement. As humans, we agree more than we disagree. Although we all have differences we have many things which are alike. We agree we need air to breathe, no one is perfect. Everyone is entitled to their own opinion. Gravity keeps us grounded. There is a time to be born and a time to die. Time waits for no one. We can agree on these basics because of life experiences, those things which have been tested and tried through our five senses.

Some things we will encounter can only be agreed upon by those, having experienced New Birth, and are a part of The Body of Christ. Not having experienced them, these beliefs may be harder for some to agree with. For now, we will remain in a state of agreement by staying on common ground. I believe, at the conclusion of this manuscript, by God's Grace, many more of us will be able to walk together in total agreement concerning great and marvelous things. There are certain principles of God operating in the earth realm, whether you are a believer or not. They just work. For example, the Law of Gravity proves what goes up must come down. The Law of Reciprocity which promises, "You reap what you sow." These are principles or the Laws of Nature (God's Creation).

The principle of agreement, when applied in every area of our lives, will crown our lives with peace (Romans 12:18). For example, your optician has informed you your glasses you ordered ten days ago are ready to be picked up. All things being normal, you throw the covers back as you reach for your robe preparing to start your day. Planting your feet, putting your body weight on the floor, your big toe on your right foot gives off a sharp pain. Surprised, you clutch your foot. The remainder of your body parts are collectively and instantaneously in sympathy with the hurting toe. Your hands reach to comfort your toe which now has your full attention. Your eyes search the area as your lips grimace in pain and your teeth clinch. Your plans change. You no longer have control of your day. Your whole focus is now on your hurting toe.

Christ is the head of the Church. He leads and guides through His Spirit. He gives directions through His Spirit and His Word. It is important that each body member is in agreement. It doesn't matter how large or small; seen or unseen, attractive or unattractive the body part is. Each has significance in the effectual functioning of the body. Unfortunately, sometimes we have missing body parts or members who are not functioning at optimum capacity. Consider the blind, the lame, the halt and the maimed; although not perfect, they are still a part of the body. Many times the strong will have to bare the infirmities of the weak (Romans 15:1). In these instances, the body learns to overcompensate, by making up for the weaker or less comely member (1 Corinthians 12:23, Exodus 4:11). Whether being compensated or compensating, all body parts are necessary and need to be a part of the agreement. We are the body of Christ. To be successful we must be in agreement with the head of the body, which is Christ (Colossians 1:24).

The principal of agreement is necessary in the world as well as in The Body of Christ.

Nothing could function without it. Thousands of decisions, large and small are made every minute of our lives, most of which we are not conscious. They are often made without challenge or controversy. You would be amazed.

When our physical body functions are not in agreement, we need a physician or a chiropractor. When we are mentally stressed or depressed we call a psychiatrists. All sicknesses and diseases would climb at an astronomical rate if unattended. Mental institutions and hospitals would be hard-pressed to facilitate and care for the infirmed population. Agreement is God's plan to bring about harmony and peace in every area of our personal lives, as well as in our society. In our country we pass civil, local, and federal laws, to enforce decisions made by those at the head of our Government.

The Kingdom of God has laws set by The King of The Kingdom, God. We don't get to vote yea or nay, we just obey. We trust that His Laws are for the good of all concerned, without exception. We are a body with many members, one being no more or less important than the other. We are to work together for the good of the whole body, with Christ as the Head (Ephesians 4:14-16). We might disagree, while never becoming disagreeable and causing schism or disorder in the body (1 Corinthians 12:14-28, KJV).

Chapter 5

You Have a Story

Frankly, I thought the scenario of the painful toe was rather catchy. I'm sure it was not as interesting as some of the stories out there. Each one of you has a story. In the church world we call it a testimony. Testimonies are the occurrences in your life that you might consider unimportant. The bible is filled with them. Your story can be great material for rightly dividing The Word.

You might be surprised how eyes would bug and mouths drop open because of the untold victories in your life. Some of which may be very similar to the lady's next door. If you were listening, you would hear her telling your whole life with *her* words. Hopefully, you are inspired to share as we cultivate our fellowship through this experience in the days, weeks, and years to come.

Why do most stories go unheard? In too many instances we hide behind masks, hoping others will approve and include us. Sometimes we feel our experiences are too shameful or embarrassing. We pretend to be perfect, without failure, and flaws. Some of us keep others at arm's length to avoid any up close and personal contact.

which inspired me while pricking my conscious through his zealous preaching.

As I attempt to complete this assignment,the Honorable Dr. Billy Graham has just completed his journey home (February 21, 2018). He has fought a good fight and, he has been faithful and obedient to the purpose for his life. God is pleased with him. So, our people were obedient as we sacrificially gave Him our only day of freedom from hard labor and our ways pleased God. My people are blessed because of it. I learned, much later, by my beloved pastor, obedience is God's Plan to reward His children. I am sure Dr. Billy Graham will be greatly rewarded for his obedience to God.

Chapter 7

Be Careful Little Eyes

We, who hunger for God's Word, are living in the season of technological advantages right at our fingertips. We are able to speak into various gadgets from across the room or in our pockets, and have them respond. We can retrieve any and everything we desire to know on the internet; some of which we would be better off not knowing. We should be especially discerning when faced with such possibly invasive technology that is available to our younger generation.

The scripture advises us to *be wise as serpents and harmless as doves,* guarding our heart with all diligence, for out of our heart (the seat of our soul) flows the issues of life.

The children sing:

"Be careful little eyes what you see... little ears what you hear..."

Everything which passes through the *gates* of our mind becomes a permanent fixture. What we see, what we hear, what we touch, and what we smell or taste are all subject to become a part of our character. The enemy, pressing the right button at the right time, can activate "pop-ups" in our brain, whether conscious or subconscious. For example, you're sitting in church when, in the middle of the preached Word, without warning, a movie scene or burger commercial pops up in your mind's eye triggering a response, a feeling, desire, action or reaction.

Once you open a door, permitting entrance, the impression gladly accepts your invitation and makes itself comfortable. It becomes a *foothold and then a stronghold*. You find there is no delete button after all (Matthew 12:29, Mark 3:26-29), Luke 11:21-26). Nothing short of deliverance will get rid of it. If after being delivered, if given a chance, it will return.(Matthew 12:43-44).

Warning! Be careful what you allow to enter into the five gates of your mind (your five senses). For example, if you are frequently exposed to profanity, whether or not you make it a personal practiced behavior, you will find profanity making an uninvited appearance when you least expect it. At some time, unaware to you, somewhere within your environment, a seed was planted in your mind. The seed of profanity has taken root and is now bringing forth it's inevitable fruit.

The enemy of our soul is always spreading seeds of erroneous doctrine and corruption in every way available. He is especially active in our airways and through all forms of communication. He is the "Prince of the air." His favorite bumper crop is the lie. He is the father of lies (John 8:44)! Whenever he speaks, he gives birth to his notorious seed.

Chapter 8

———◆———

Beware of the Lie

It is often heard, "What you don't know won't hurt you." Oh Really?

Much to the contrary, the prophet Hosea, whom many have labeled a *minor* prophet for some reason, warns:

"My people are destroyed for lack of knowledge" (Hosea 4:6).

Lack of knowledge carries with it an arsenal of few, but deadly weapons. It is always necessary to arm ourselves with knowledge. It is a powerful defensive weapon in spiritual warfare. We are no longer defenseless and made subject to the enemy's limited devices.

Not only is the devil limited in his ability to defeat us, but he uses our cooperation to be effective.

We often provide him with assistance through our ignorance. The less we know, the more we aid the enemy in accomplishing his diabolical assignments against us. For example, 911 and the enemy's attack on our land used *our* resources to train, kill, and destroy. Many times we are the ones aiding and abetting the enemy. The Apostle Paul admonishes us *not to be ignorant of our enemy's devices,* the most effective of which are, *ignorance, doubt, fear, and unbelief.* Diligently studying and *rightly dividing the Word of Truth* draws us nearer to the Savior while building our defenses against the enemy and his tactics.

John 10:10a clearly defines the enemy's trajectory by opposing the promise of our Lord and Savior, Jesus Christ (John 10:10b). The thief comes only to steal, kill and destroy. He has come to trip us by causing us to stray from the protective realm of the promise of abundant life decreed in the later part of this scripture.

There is no limit to the enemy's efforts to deceive the believer as well as the non believer.

He tempted Jesus as he hungered in the wilderness. He uses temptation, deception, and lies. He intentionally misuses scripture (Psalm 91:11, Matthew 4:6). Learning scriptures and hiding them in our hearts increases our defenses against every enemy device, thus rendering them of non-effect. Careful observation, plus diligent application, assures you the enemy is powerless (Matthew 28:18, Isaiah 54:17, Luke 10:19, and 1 Corinthians 15:55).

His plans and schemes are only as effective as *we* allow. The power belongs to Jesus who returned it to us through the work on Calvary's Cross. If the enemy lied to Jesus (Matthew 4), he will certainly lie to us.

The following statement may come as a surprise to some. It might even sound like blasphemy or heresy.

Everything in scripture is accurate and explicit in content, but not everything recorded in scripture is true!

Does this sound confusing?

Allow me to elaborate. Satan is not the only one recorded as lying in scripture. There are many recorded lies, untruths, and desceptions recorded in the Holy Word. This is a subject seldom addressed by theologians and Bible teachers. It is very important to know when rightly dividing The Word of Truth, especially amongst babes desiring THE SINCERE MILK! There are accurate recordings of several characters in scripture, other than the liar himself, who have told untruths, i.e. Abraham, Isaac, Jacob, Rahab, and King Saul, to name a few. The recording of Job's friends who made accusations against him, as well as against God, which, if *rightly divided*, proves my point. God had much to say about Job's friends exchange at the end of the book of Job. In the concluding chapter, God sets them *all* straight. Job's friends had to apologize to him and Job had to apologize to God; whose word is forever without error.

The Bible is not provided to win fans or favor but that the absolute Truth might be told of accurate occurrences in times past, as well as prophesy of what will occur in the future.

You don't have to consult soothe sayers and *"Horror- scope"* predictions to know what will happen in the future. The loving, just and equitable God, who, throughout the Old Testament, is revealing His plan for all believers in the legal document we call the Bible:

Basic Instructions Before Leaving Earth.

Chapter 9

Importance of Context

When studying The written Word (Logos), it is very important to consider the WHO, WHAT, WHERE, and WHEN.

There is also the HOW and WHY to be considered, but are among the seldom disclosed context of God's Wisdom (Job 38-40). You may often accurately discover Who, What, Where and When; but not often are we able to discern Why and How.

The BIBLE contains the Constitution or Kingdom Laws revealed to the citizens of The Kingdom, courtesy of The King. The context of the Word of God is in sync with various periods that we refer to as Dispensations. There are differences of opinion among theologians as to how many original Dispensations exist. There are as few as three and as many as seven.

The names of Dispensations differ also. (WIKIPEDIA)

The only three things these varied schools of thought unquestionably reveal are:

1. We know in part.
2. God alone is all-knowing, or Omniscient.
3. The more we know the more we realize we don't know.

For clarity we will engage five Dispensations:

1. Dispensation of Innocence (absence of Sin)
2. Dispensation of Conscience (knowing right from wrong)
3. Dispensation of The Law, (of Moses)
4. Dispensation of Grace (The Church of Christ)
5. Dispensation of The Fullness of Time (end of the age) (WIKIPEDIA)

Knowing which Dispensation the scripture is reflecting or is occurring helps in rightly dividing The Word. The Word of God is recorded in alignment with the Dispensation or Administration of God in operation relevant to the time in which it was recorded.

Be assured, God's Word never changes. His Administration and Dispensation, or how He handles or administrates does change, according to His Divine Wisdom, His predestined will, and His foreknowledge. God's Will has been established. He makes no last minute changes. Every Word is already settled (Psalm 119:89-96).

Acts 10 is a perfect example of an obvious shift in Dispensations.

(Read Acts 10:9-48). These scriptures give us an on-the-spot observance as God transfers Peter from The Dispensation of The Law into another Dispensation called, The Church or Grace, established through the crucifixion and resurrection of Christ.

Not only is it important to know WHO said it, but WHEN it was said,

WHAT was happening and WHERE it was said.

Professing content without context is pretense.

Using these reminders might help to recognize the 'When' of the content:

O.T. = Old Testament
N.T. = New Testament
B.C. = Before Crucifixion
A.C. = After Crucifixion
B.R. = Before Resurrection
A.R. = After Resurrection

While these abbreviations are not authentic, but personal, they might serve to provide a significant tool while rightly dividing The Word. I have found this information applicable to most scripture text. For example, the Old Testament scripture Ezekiel 18:20 states:

"The soul that sinneth it shall die."

This decree was given under The Dispensation of the Law in the O.T. under which Jesus was born. Nevertheless, He, Jesus, is found pointing to the N.T. scripture and The Dispensation of Grace (The Church), prophetically declaring believers in HIM shall never die (John 11:25-26). His death would usher in The New Dispensation A.C.; thereby, replacing The Dispensation of The Law B.C.. While scripture taken from Ezekiel is not a lie, it becomes of non-effect in light of the change in Dispensation (Administration).

I emphasize caution when studying the writings of King Solomon in the book of Ecclesiastes. Applying the correct context is crucial. Much of what Solomon says in an apparent state of frustration and despair is not to be trusted as sound doctrine, but tainted by the consequences of his fall from grace due to covetousness. When did he say it? What was happening? Where was he when he said it?

Unfortunately Solomon was influenced by his many wives, Pharaoh's daughter being the first (1King 10:13). Solomon had a harem of over1000 concubines and lovers, many who were idol worshippers. He made treaties with The Egyptians, which was against Torah Law. His many egregious acts alienated him from the favor of God. He left following after The True God, the source of his wisdom, choosing to chase after material wealth (1 Kings 10:23 25). His final lament is recorded in Ecclesiastes 12, as he approaches the end of his life, finally admitting the vanity he pursued in his youth. Seeming to have much regret, Solomon acknowledges the futility of his ways. He is trying to save us through his experience from a "wouda, couda, shouda" experience.

As mentioned earlier WHO, WHAT, WHERE and WHEN often allow conclusive evidence; however, WHY and HOW are rarely revealed. For example, the feeding of the 5,000, Manna from heaven for over forty years, Daniel in the lion's den, the three Hebrew boys, and lastly, Peter's walking on water. Without a prescribed approach, having little evidence in such instances, we are left without a choice but to attribute such occurrences to the *miraculous* and/or *the supernatural*.

Chapter 10

Doubtful Disputations

Not walking in agreement leaves room for a greater disruption in the Body of Christ, some of which the Bible labels "Doubtful Disputations" (Romans 14:1-10). What are they?

Briefly, *doubtful disputations* are seemingly *ambiguous* scriptures within the text, that aren't easily distinguishable or without clear meaning. This often allows for different interpretations of the text. For example, David stated in Psalm 37:25:

"I have been young and now I am old yet I've never seen the righteous forsaken nor his seed begging bread."

This scripture can be interpreted in different ways. There may be other views of this scripture that have opposing thought patterns with each view supported by scripture.

Let's look closely.

We begin by studying the context surrounding the scripture. Do we know WHO is speaking? Can we discern WHEN and WHERE it was said? WHAT was happening at the time it was said?

Contextual evidence may or may not be pronounced, but we begin looking for them within the content.

WHAT do *you* believe David is saying?:

I have lived a long time and God has never allowed me to suffer abandonment or go without food (Psalm 23).

Or is David saying...

All my life, as it has been within my power, I have never neglected to provide for God's people, but always meeting their needs. (2 Samuel 9:1-3).

In these instances, each student/believer has opposing opinions accompanied by what is believed to be supporting scriptures. Which one is correct?

In the final analysis, while trying to conclude, there are things one should first consider:

1. Is the scripture in question vital to one's salvation?
2. Is the scripture regarding a life or death decision?

If we agree that the answer to these two questions is a resounding no, we have found a place on which to agree to disagree. We never become disagreeable, but move on, allowing The Holy Spirit to clarify, or not clarify, through prayer or revelation. He is able to provide excellent counsel. Opposing views are never a reason to break or bruise fellowship.

DISPUTATION! Notice the inner word *dispute.*

Many times these disputes have birthed multiple denominations, scattering the body of Christ; a divide and conquer tactic of the enemy (Matthew 12:22-25)). We are then unable to combine forces, gifts, and strengths; as each denomination goes into pride-driven modes and agendas.

There is nothing recorded in scripture concerning denominations. These are *man generated* through arrogance, ignorance, and pride. God is not pleased and does not operate according to these concepts. If He doesn't allow us to consider male, female, Greek or Jew, then there are certainly no denominational differences. Jesus has broken down the wall of partition) by His crucifixion (Ephesians 2:14).

Most denominational, as well as religious dogma, is identified with names related to a man or woman's personal ministry, a movement or church congregation (a person, place or thing) i.e.: Baptist, COGIC, Holy Ghost Headquarters, Pentecostal, Apostolic, Methodist, Holiness, Presbyterian, Episcopalian, Azusa Street, and other practices and theologies. They are too numerous to name. There is never just cause to become disagreeable because of differences of opinions. This mindset promotes confusion and discord, particularly in the Church, as well in family relationships. Stubborn arrogance and pride are at the root of this age-old confusion. More accurately, it is the same enemy who promotes lies and pride which causes confusion. God is not the author of confusion!

There is always common ground on which to stand, thereby, securing the bond of peace. Upon finding that place, we move ahead, never compromising Truth, not even for the sake of agreement. There is one church and that is the Church of Jesus Christ. He is the founder and the builder (Matthew 16:15-20). The effective weapon of our warfare, that guarantees the enemy's sure defeat, is unity (Genesis 11:1-9, Matthew 12:22-28, and Galatians 3:28).

Chapter 11

—◆—

Wisdom From Above

No matter one's ethnicity, socioeconomic status, or educational achievement, God's Word has no respect of persons. Whosoever will let him ask for God's wisdom.

The Word tells us to get wisdom and with that get understanding. James says if you lack wisdom, ask and God will give it without reprimanding you for not knowing (James 1:5). The scriptures invites us to Ask, Seek, and Knock (Matthew 7:7).

Be warned! There is earthly wisdom as well as Godly Wisdom, each having a different path (James 3:13-18). Spending quality time with God, through His Word, and with The Holy Spirit is a sure way to acquire The Wisdom of God, as well as secure your focus on the path prepared by God. The earthly wisdom is comprised of man's leaning and his finite understanding; therefore, he is unable to reveal God's heavenly mysteries. We can begin on the path of godly wisdom but become detoured if we are not led by The Spirit (Proverbs 14:12).

Jesus invites us to take His yoke upon us and learn of Him. To become intimately related to The Father is one sure way of receiving wisdom from above. The more time invested the greater the dividends. Such determined positioning provides access into the storehouse of The Omniscient God. Nothing will be impossible when you know in your knower that your information is God approved (2 Timothy 2:15). Your confidence becomes unshakeable the more familiar you become with, not only *what God* does, but knowing what pleases Him (Psalm 103:7).

Omniscience (Omni-Science) another of God's spiritual attributes, simply means He is the source of all wisdom. He is all wise, all knowing, the source of every witty invention, from the beginning to the end of time and throughout eternity (Proverbs 8:12; John 1:3).

I would be totally remiss in neglecting to mention the Third Member of The Godhead, The Holy Spirit, to whom God reveals all things. The Holy Spirit in turn reveals them to us at the opportune time and season, through study, prayer, fasting, and meditation. He is somewhat akin to a spiritual transformer. The Holy Spirit receives and makes intercession, transferring God's Wisdom to our finite brain. Without Him making intercession for us, receiving information directly from God would be too implosive for our frail beings. Realizing we are finite, He translates the things of God so we can relate and understand.

We often see the use of "as of" to compare a familiar term to the content and the context of what can be otherwise unfamiliar in scripture content (Acts 2:2-4, Revelation 1:10, 9:1-12). As a result, we have a conduit into The Mind of Christ! (Romans 8: 26, 1 Corinthians 2:16). The Holy Spirit is also our intercessor (conduit) when we don't know what to pray for (Romans 8:26-28) or what to say.

Chapter 12

————◆————

The Power of Knowledge

A jingle heard in my early childhood left an impression which obviously stuck. I believe it was the theme song of an old radio quiz show which chanted:

'It pays to be ignorant, to be dumb, to be dense, to be ignorant. It pays to be ignorant just like me".

That's a lie straight from the pit of Hell!

We agreed earlier that knowledge is powerful, but with the wrong intent it can also be destructive. The enemy attempts to keep us happy in our ignorance; causing us to believe it is better not to know. He wants us to believe ignorance is bliss! More lies! What you don't know will indeed hurt you as well as keep you held captive (2 Timothy 2:24-26).

Seek intimacy with Our Father as early as possible. The sooner you do the less regrets you will have at any age. The proper investment of time is most productive in establishing a deep and meaningful relationship with God. Endeavor to spend quality time with Him, the giver of all good and perfect gifts (James 1:17).

To know God is to love Him. To love Him is to desire Him.

An increasing desire for fellowship with The Savior must become our daily bread, and our spiritual food. As we would not go without natural food, we must daily digest the Word of God at an increasing level, three times daily plus snacks.

Beginning our day in God's presence through thanksgiving,worship and praise; entering by The Word is true wisdom. Remember, *NO BIBLE, NO BREAKFAST! The* 'Psalmist expresses The Word of God as being his soul food. As we hunger and thirst after righteousness,The Holy Spirit helps us digest line upon line. As babes we should desire *The Sincere Milk* of the word. He, The Holy Spirit is totally committed to our spiritual growth and development. Invite Him in as you prepare to partake, proceeding your time in the scriptures with prayer (Psalm 119:8).

Unfortunately some of us have not been very selective in our dietary choices due to lack of knowledge. Some have been eating *religious junk food,* takeout meals, and fast foods. As a result, our spirit man is sickly and weak, some "falling asleep" before they need to (1 Corinthians 11:30).

We must be both mindful and watchful of our food intake as well as knowing who's serving. We should not partake from every table (Matthew. 6:24). Garbage in garbage out! We truly are what we eat!

Examine the contents and prove the context. Try all spirits with the written Word. Discern what spirit is behind what is being spoken, sung, preached, or written. Here is how you try the spirit to see that it is of God (1 John 4:1-5). Ask the Holy Spirit:

Does what I am feeling match up with The Word of God?

Is what I am doing, saying, or listening to pleasing to God?

Is what I am eating or drinking pleasing to God?

Would I do it if God were visibly with me?

Give it the taste test. Read it for yourself. If you doubt it, pray about it.

Emulate the Bereans in the early church (Acts 17:11).

Let God be true and every man a liar (Romans. 3:4). Don't take anyone's word to be true. Trust and believe God's Word in its proper context.

Taste and see for yourself.

Chapter 13

———◆———

Good Ground

I believe the ground has been properly prepared, because we have been made aware of certain keys necessary to rightly divide The Word.

Those of us who have been Born of The Spirit are fully equipped with all we need, The Word (His legal Will) and The Spirit of God. You now possess new wineskins. You are able to receive the new wine (Matthew. 9: 14-17).

Your development and maturity will increase with application (use) and experience (James 1:22-25). You are ready to begin this great adventure of rightly dividing God's Word. Our focus will be the first three chapters of the book of Genesis.

As the name implies, Genesis introduces us to the very beginning of all things created (John 1:3).

I pray that the application of this book will help create a desire to go deeper into the Holy Scriptures wherein awaits intrigue, mysteries, miracles, and supernatural occurrences far beyond our finite imagination. With all the advances in our modern technological environment, The Holy Bible still remains the number one bestseller of all books written.

Chapter 14

—◆—

An Open Invitation

To all greatly honored Watchmen of the Faith, as well as protectors of the sacred Constitution of The Kingdom of God; I respectfully acknowledge your having repeatedly read these sacred scrolls. Nevertheless, I invite you to come join us on this exciting and rare look behind the scenes of the beginning. You might be surprised by the new discoveries you will find much to our mutual delight. One of many fascinating aspects of the Word of God is discovering new facets which become ours to possess. Just when we think we've seen all there is to see, know all there is to know, having been illumined again and again, VOILA, up pops a fresh and new awareness.

The Master Teacher, The Holy Spirit, the Third Person of The Godhead, The One who embraced the Spiritual Baton as Jesus said from the cross, "Into thy hands I commend my Spirit," shows us things we've never before seen or understood. This same Holy Spirit who Christ promised to send to us, (which He did) comes in, lovingly leading us into another promise. (John 14:7-18, MSG). We follow The Holy Spirit as He follows Christ. He never speaks of Himself, but speaks only what God tells Him to speak.

Let us break and partake of this Fresh Bread together.

We welcome you!

Chapter 15

Bible Study

We will take time to carefully deliberate over the Logos, written Word, while praying for The Rhema which is the Living Word. It is our belief, Jesus himself, will manifest, (show up), giving us a right now Word (Matthew.18:18-20, MSG). Jesus is always attentive when we make Him the center of all we undertake for His name's sake. He is pleased with our fellowship! (Malachi 3:16-18)

It is so important to have a Bible translation that is easy for you to understand. Let me recommend a parallel Bible that has at least two different, side by side, translations.

Your method of study might vary. There are different methods of studying The Bible. You might prefer a Topical Study Bible, wherein you choose a topic, for example, "faith," and then, using a concordance of your choice, find scriptures about faith. You might want a bible written in chronological order. Perhaps you want Bible prophecies, or Promises of God highlighted within the pages. These are all available online.

You might be one who randomly flips the pages and begins reading wherever you find yourself. This method might be suitable for a casual

ELDERMARGE

"on the go" scripture, but not highly recommended for exhaustive Bible Study.

A quiet place with good lighting and perhaps soft worship music might be nice. Be careful not to get too comfortable, inducing the spirit of slumber which is often used by our enemy.

There is reading The Bible for information and there is reading for your intimate pleasure. Both are equally rewarding. It is good to read scripture many times over, enabling you to commit them to your memory. You will be blessed as you receive a deeper understanding with each rereading of familiar scripture.

It is advisable to add a Bible Dictionary and a Bible Concordance to your study tools. There are many from which to choose. What really matters is that the reader understands what he or she is reading. There are many translations, even transliterations on the internet, enabling you to view and compare. The Bible Hub and Bible Gateway have many versions from which to choose. Your local bookstore attendant might be able to help you find the right Bible to meet your satisfaction.

In my opinion, nothing beats a good old hands-on hard copy of your choice; wherein you can make personal notations, highlight your favorite scriptures, dog ear the pages, etc. It is often noted that a well worn Bible is a positive indication of a well lived life Let us pray before we eat!

Heavenly Father,

We invite You to lead us in this precious fellowship.

You said where two or more are gathered in Your name there You would be in the midst; so here we are to worship and praise You for Your goodness and Your mercy towards us. Were it not for Your tender mercies, we would be consumed.

Surely all have fallen short of your glory.

We thank You that You take time to care for us as disobedient as we are at times. You so graciously forgive us and cleanse us over and over again. We thank You, We love You.

Receive this humble offering and glorify our time together. We bring You our offering asking You to multiply it so that we might have to share with those who hunger and thirst after Your Righteousness. Feed us Heavenly Father with Your precious Bread of Life.

It is in Your Matchless Name we pray,

Amen

Chapter 16

——◆◆◆——

It's a Faith Walk

My spirit bears witness to what I have read in scripture that the first five books of the bible, known as the Pentateuch, were written by Moses, a man mightily used of God.

I am not trying to reinvent the wheel. Everything I hold as Truth. Moses is referred to as a friend of God and is also identified as God's Prophet. He is recorded as having to have spoken with God face to face (Exodus 33:11).

The scripture reveals Moses spent quality, as well as, quantity time in the Presence of God. There was a time recorded in scripture, he was forty days and nights in God's Presence.on a mountain without food or drink. At the end of the 40 days, he returned carrying two tablets of stone on which was written The Ten commandments, scripted by the fiery finger of God Himself!

Having been in God's presence, Moses' face is said to have become extremely radiant. It was so much so, that Moses was asked to veil his face (2 Corinthians 3:16). The scripture indicates it was Moses' curious nature which led to his first recorded encounter with God. Should we continue the fellowship beyond the Book of Exodus we will learn more. Details that are not revealed in scripture remain a mystery. For example, how was Moses able to record what happened before he was born? Were there other long periods of time Moses spent alone with God that are not recorded in scripture?

You might want to make a note of questions you desire to have answered.

Perhaps The Holy Spirit can answer questions for you in your private prayer time or in times of meditation.

Pastors have a way of addressing questions within their sermons without realizing you were looking for a particular answer. Amazing! There are times when you get the impression your pastor is reading your thoughts!

There may be some who find scripture difficult to understand. You are certainly not alone.This is true, more often than not, with babes as well as seasoned saints. That is perfectly fine. We are not going to understand every jot and every tittle found in scripture.

Read and put into practice what you do understand,and pray about what you do not. Keep a pen, pencil, paper,a highlighter, a bible dictionary, and a concordance handy. Make notes as you read and questions arise. Prayerfully you will remain intrigued, even eager to learn that which is written as well as those things which are implied.

Unfortunately there are people who will simply refuse to believe much of what is written in the Holy Scriptures. This is a critically unfortunate position to maintain. Our belief system is of major importance to our growth. One's belief system is the primary thing which separates the children of The Kingdom of God from the world systems (Hebrews.11:6). Curiosity can lead to a healthy inquisition that causes one to search the scriptures with a zeal for knowledge. Unbelief, on the contrary, is a deadly affliction from the enemy, causing stumbling blocks and preventing one from accepting the free gift of salvation. Unbelief is, and will forever be, the gulf fixed between God's Kingdom Children and the children being held captive (2 Timothy 3:24). Keep in mind there are two kingdoms. All of us are the children of one or the other.

We often come across truth which seems hard to believe; however, we cannot choose which scripture to believe, or accept, or to obey.

After studying the content of the scripture (see Chapter 9 Importance of Context), we must discern its veracity, (truth) it's virtue, to discover the validation of God's Word. Ask yourself the question, does this statement agree with other scriptures?

Your new spirit man will bear witness with what is true and reject that which is not. You must believe that which is proven to agree with God's Word. Whether you doubt or are undecided, you must let your spirit man, who is being led by the Holy Spirit, lead you (1st Corinthians 2:14, 2nd Corinthians 4:3-4, MSG).

Rightly dividing the Word of Truth should never be an attempt at proving yourself correct, instead it is allowing the Holy Spirit to teach sound doctrine according to The Word of God. Let the proverbial *chips* fall where they may.

Your belief system will determine your growth in the process of Rightly Dividing The Word of Truth. If you are having difficulty believing Genesis chapter 1, 2, and 3, you will certainly have trouble believing the recordings of Jonah and the big fish or the witness of The Three Hebrew Boys (Daniel 3).

Do not systematically avoid passages which you find difficult to understand. You must realize all scripture is important, whether we understand them or not. Remember to make a note of, or highlight scripture you find complicated as a reminder to revisit them for further study.

Jesus said,

"Blessed is he who hungers and thirsts after righteousness, they shall be filled." (Matthew 5:6) That's a promise. Don't be discouraged.

Chapter 17

———◆———

Questions Anyone?

As we approach Genesis 1:1, we see that in the beginning was God.

Not only was He in the beginning, He IS The Beginning.

I worked at a local television broadcasting center for a short while. One of the featured programs called *Ask The Pastor, allowed the opportunity for questions to be asked by viewers. Visiting pastors were invited to answer the questions which were presented.* Some of the questions were very basic, but vital. Someone seasoned in The Word might consider them nonsensical. During this experience I was made aware of the importance of every question. There are no ridiculous questions, as some might suppose. All questions should be addressed, especially those expressing a sincere desire to know. There is no question undeserving of an answer. No one is ever too old or too young to make earnest inquiries. Questions are positive tools in reaching believers. Jesus used them very skillfully while searching their thoughts and intents of the heart. Callers have been known to ask questions such as:

Who made God?

Questions answered properly will help to form a firm foundation needed by each individual. Questions improperly answered are able to prevent such a foundation from being formed. The unadulterated Word of God is mandatory in each individual relationship with God, and is only established through searching the scriptures (God's Word). There is no substitute. Only then will you be able to endure the hard times guaranteed to come to every believer (Matthew 7:24-27).

No question should go unanswered, even if the reply is *"I don't know"* or *"Let's search it out together."* Either response is better than no answer. 'I don't know' is an honest reply that is void of deceit or confusion. Some questions may seem to be child-like. Jesus reminds us that unless we come as a child we cannot enter into The Kingdom (Mark 10:13-15,MSG.). This is not referring to a chronological age, but to a state of mind, having no hypocrisy, or attitude. One should have an open heart, trusting and ready to receive sound instruction; void of malice or an ulterior motive. We should never ask or engage questions for the purpose of debate or strife (2 Timothy 2:24). If it becomes obvious to us that someone has such an intent simply respond by saying "I'm not striving with you." End of discussion!

What about God's origin? God has natural attributes, as well as spiritual ones or characteristics. Self-Existence is one of His spiritual attributes. No one made or created God. He is self-existent; which often causes many to stumble. His existence is within Himself.

Another one of His spiritual attributes is that He is eternal. He Is, was, and will always be eternal! You might argue, that these responses fall short of a concrete explanation, and in fact, does not explain anything to the satisfaction of an inquiring mind. You can't Google it or look it up on Wikipedia. To that I say conclusively, if we were able to explain these attributes of God, we would *BE GOD,* and we would have *need* of God.

Chapter 18

You Must Be Born Again

Should you choose to cultivate this opportunity being made available to everyone through this manuscript you must understand it is only possible through mutual love for The Father, and built on faith in Him. It can only be received accordingly (Hebrew 11:1-6). This unique relationship begins through the ability to believe and receive by way of a born again spirit man.

As it was explained in the Preface of this manuscript,we were born in sin through no fault of our own. Unless you are Born Again of God's Spirit, you cannot, nor will you ever be able to receive or understand the things of God, as they are spiritually discerned (1 Corinthians 2:14). You must be born of His Spirit in order to understand these things which are written throughout the scriptures. (John 3:3-8, 1ˢᵗ Corinthians 2:9 -16).

This absolute truth, is never subject to change, though it might often sound redundant and repetitive. This knowledge is important and warrants repeating. We cannot be saved from the wages of sin (Romans 6:23) any other way! Anyone who thinks otherwise will be "out" at home base.

For example, If I were to clothe a thoroughbred canine in a designer suit and tie, provide it with an attaché case, drive him to the nearest municipal building, place him in a seat at the council table in a court of law and expect him, as my attorney, to plead my case, I would be declared insane.

The natural man, expecting to discern godly things would be declared equally insane (1 Corinthians 2:11-16). The spirit of the natural man knows only the things of a natural man. We all must be born of the Spirit of God to know and understand the things of God. We need a new beginning, a new spirit man. The Old Testament saints who tried to live in Holy obedience needed The Gospel preached to them after the resurrection of Christ in order to receive a new spirit (1 Peter 3:19-20).

My reiteration of this very important bit of information might seem overly expressed. That is intentionally so! This point is too important to be taken lightly! If you were to read this book cover to cover, and go away not recognizing this one important fact, it would indeed be a travesty. Miss this and YOU'RE OUT! Eternally!

Please! Do not misunderstand. This relationship is never one which is commandeered. The Godhead will not drag anyone kicking and screaming, into His Kingdom. God created us from the beginning with a 'free will'. You are never asked to relinquish your ability to choose. God doesn't intend for you to become a clone or a robot. He has an initial stipulation concerning our eternal life, you must be born again (John 3:3). The choice yet remains completely yours; however, and make no mistake about this one thing, the consequences belong to God alone. You do not get to choose this one. He does. It's called The Final Judgement (Matthew 25:46, Hebrews 9:27, Revelation 20:11-15).

Whether you believe or not does not change the consequences of your choice. By not choosing you choose by default. Even If you skip this part of the manuscript it does not change. The Truth will make you free.

Everyone will be given a choice in one way or another, by some one or another, at one time or another. You have been told and the choice is up to you. The important difference between Kingdom Citizens and those who choose to remain "aliens from The Promise" (Ephesians 2:12) are quite simple. Those who have accepted the gift of salvation are no longer controlled by their sinful inclinations which tugs at their fleshly nature. Kingdom Citizens now have the power to say *no* to the old man's desires and yes to the new born again man in us; which is eternal (John 1:11).

Kingdom Citizens are no longer held captive without choices. We still have to choose, but we now have the power to choose life (Deuteronomy 30:15-20). New Life begins and never ends the moment we choose to say YES!

We all will constantly be required to make such choices as the spiritual battle for souls, hearts, and minds continues to rage. Trying to tempt us on every side, the enemy is persistent in his efforts to regain and restore our allegiance to his kingdom of darkness, from which we are set free.

Having a Born Again spirit is the only way we can stand against the enemy of our souls, who is constantly trying to defeat us.(John 10:10a) Without the miraculous occurance of the new birth we are helpless against the lies and schemes. Everything we receive with the gift of salvation is given to help us in the natural as well as the spiritual. The supernatural occurrences are inevitable in our lives. No amount of intelligence can provide this protection (Psalms 41:6).

The bible is a book full of supernatural occurrences and peculiar events. There are many mysteries within its pages. The Apostle Paul often speaks of the mysteries of God, some of which he, along with the other inspired writers of the Gospels, (2 Timothy 3:16) share while others remain mysteries (Ephesians 1:9, Deuteronomy 29:29). It seems The Apostle Paul is given permission to share one such mystery beginning in 1st Corinthians 15:52 and another in 2nd Corinthians, the 12th chapter. Read the aforementioned scriptures to see how Paul cautiously offers insight into these very important events.

The scriptures, the Born-again believers are privileged to possess, are given for our information and example. They are not given just to train us and prepare us for Kingdom Living and Eternal Life, but they are given to help maintain possession of the victorious and abundant life we have received through Christ's Victory on the Cross, (John 10:10b) which is available here and now. The scriptures promise a reward of life throughout eternity (2 Timothy 3:16, Ephesians 5:25-26, 6:18, Colossians. 3:1-3).

The Bible also serve as examples to be followed by every child of God in order that we might live a life pleasing to God. In reality, the scriptures are actual testimonies of those who have gone before us, those having had real life experiences resulting from their obedience and faith in God (Hebrews 12:1-2).

Jesus' Sermon on the Mount, popularly called, *The Beatitudes, are* a complete portrait of the attitude and presence of mind Kingdom Children should labor to develop and maintain. We are being transformed (Romans 12:1-3) into Our God's Image and likeness as it was in the Beginning (Genesis 1:26). The *Beatitudes promote* an ongoing self-examination (James 1:14).

The Bible very uniquely verifies itself in melodious tones played throughout both the Old and New Testament, although it had been written hundreds of years apart. We find an uninterrupted symphony from Genesis to Revelation.

The more you determine to indulge in this love relationship with The Father the more prevalent this melodious refrain begins to persuade you of its authenticity and validity (Romans 8: 38-39). Mysteries become less mysterious. Things begin to fall into place as a giant heavenly puzzle unfolding age old hidden treasures. As we study, things which were once just *"hearsay"* are now becoming persuasive to a maturing child of Faith, while non-believers become more hardened of heart as if tone deaf.

Faith comes by hearing and hearing by the Word of God. Do you hear what I hear? The more you hear and apply that which you hear, the more you become the word made flesh, Sons of God, for whom the whole creation is groaning and travailing waiting for us to come forward taking dominion once again (Romans 8:22). We become doers of The Word, operating in Kingdom Authority, able to provide much needed solutions to those in need.

Help is always at hand as we partake of the scriptures daily. The Holy Spirit comes in and sets up a virtual classroom in our hearts, with illustrious past, present, and future insight as only He does (John 16:13, 1John 2:27). We need The Spirit of God in order to understand the things of God! (1 Corinthians 2:9-12) We now understand His Word made universal by His Spirit (Psalm 19:2-4). There is simply no other way to understand The Bible (John 10:27-28). Being born again is a win-win opportunity for all who will receive.

Chapter 19

———•◆•———

What Is His Name?

The bible declares in Romans l0 9:13 "Those who call upon the name of The Lord, shall be saved."

When speaking of the initial process of Salvation, The Bible declares in Acts 4:12 "...the name of Jesus is the only name whereby men must be saved."

During our study we will encounter many names by which we generally use when referring to God. As we will observe, when the scriptures record His name it is often relevant to how He is moving in the life of a specific individual.

For example, when David calls Him *His Shepherd in Psalm 23,* He is Jehovah-Rohi. When He spared Issac, Abraham's only son substituted by the ram in the bush (Genesis 17), He was Abraham's Jehovah-Jireh. His name takes on contextual relevance, having personal application according to what and who He *is* to you, as well as what He *does* for you in your hour of need. The creator told Moses, he was to refer to Him as: The "I Am That I Am". Whatever you need Him to be at the time you need Him to be, He Is that for you. All we have to do is give Him permission to take care of your need by calling on Him in prayer.

I have not found written anywhere in scripture The Creator of the Universe issued a prerequisite or decree as to what name anyone seeking salvation is to call Him in order to receive the free gift. NOWHERE! One's iIndividual ethnicity need not abandon their native tongue or dialect to receive acceptance from The Almighty God.

Our Father knows us from afar and is acquainted with every one of us. As it is written, He knows our very thoughts and even the words on our tongues before we speak them. We are written on the very palm of His Hand (Isaiah 49:16; Psalm 17:8). We are the Apple of His eye. He loves us unconditionally! He has shed His love abroad in our hearts. Paul says we can call Him "Abba" (Daddy), an intimate term of endearment.

In Philippians chapter two it is recorded that The Father has exalted Jesus by His own Authority, and has given Him a name that is above every name (Philippians 2:9). He has decreed that at the name of Jesus, every knee will bow and every tongue confess that Jesus is Lord.

It is noted by many learned theologians and those who are well versed in the Hebrew tongue that the word 'God," which we see in chapter one of Genesis, as well as throughout scripture, is the plural masuline form and is God's name' Elohim; having a masculine gender which is the entire Godhead; God The Father, God The Son and God The Holy Spirit.

Chapter 20

———◆◆◆———

Here We Go!

Please be aware that we are stepping knee deep into rightly dividing The Word of Truth from this point on. Throughout your study of The Bible always pray for discernment which comes through studying The Word of God. The more you study, the greater your discernment develops. It is a part of the gift of The Holy Spirit (Hebrews 4:12). Applying the Word sharpens our discernment.

In the very first verse, The Godhead, is acknowledged as being present in the beginning. As we continue, scriptures will corroborate this conclusion (John 1: 1-14. Colossians l.1-17). Elohim, God The creator, is at work in Genesis 1:1. God The Spirit is identified in verse two as it is said of Him to 'brood,' (Genesis 1:2,MSG) acknowledging The Spirit as having a personality as well as feelings and emotions. Therefore, we must never refer to The Holy Spirit as it, but as He, Him or His.

So far we have evidence of two persons of the Godhead. The Three in one. The Triune God!

As we study, we will see evidence of the Third part of the Godhead, The Holy Spirit. We have heard these three referred to as The Trinity. Although commonly spoken of in sermons and bible lessons, the word

'Trinity' never appears in scripture. The three together is sometimes referred to as the Triune God. (Note both words beginning with 'Tri, the prefix indicating three).

The concept of The Trinity is beyond our finite comprension, to say the least. As you become familiar with the volume of The Book, through faith and by the guidance of The Holy Spirit, you will witness the Unity of The Godhead displayed throughout The Scriptures (Hebrew 10:7).

Many have tried; in their own way, to break it down to a simple level of understanding. Some explanations serve to move us a little closer, perhaps. For example, a married man is a husband, a father, and a son. Water has three forms: liquid, solid as well as vapor. An egg is a yolk, a shell, and the white, all separate, yet one. These are pretty good examples; however it takes the Holy Spirit Himself to reveal to your spirit the reality of the Divine Unity of the GodHead. Three in One separate yet equal, each having a unique personality and function.

As you continue the earnest study of the scriptures this supernatural Three in One Person will present Himself to you personally; thereby, removing all doubt. The book of Genesis reports the beginning manifested presence of the Godhead (Genesis 1:1-3). God is in the beginning, The Spirit is in the beginning, and is said to brood over the deep; but where is God the Son? (See John 1:1) Matthew 3:16-17 gives a distinct report of the Godhead operating in unity.

May I suggest you re-read verse three, where the context finds God, The Son, speaking before He was made flesh (John 1:14). There are things recorded in the Logos, and also many things are implied. As you rightly divide The Word of truth, you will witness many such illuminations in scripture.

One scripture which remains unexplained that I believe to be worth mentioning, is the fact that in the beginning the earth is recorded as being *without form and void* (Genesis 1:2). Some theologians conclude a catastrophic occurrence took place between verses one and two of Genesis 1. God later tells the man and woman to *'replenish'* the earth; therefore, there is a connotation of something having been in place before there was a beginning, as we understand it. So, the question may be, if the world was without form and void, what was there for Adam and Eve to replenish?

While that is worth pondering, when rightly dividing the Word, we must steer clear of speculations, conjectures suppositions, hyperbole, hypothesis, and the like. We don't speculate as to what God means. There may be a vast difference between what God means and what we understand Him to mean when using the words *'without form and void'*.

It could very well mean exactly what is written, formless and of no use.

We can only be sure of that which God reveals to us by His Word and by His Spirit. Someone may have very well received Divine Revelation or Illumination to which I do not have access. I don't dispute things in those categories, neither do I teach it as Gospel! (Deut. 29:29) My rule of thumb is, if you don't know please say, *I DON'T KNOW*. What we can be sure of is that the earth was without form and void simply because it is written vas such. God has been in control of the universe since the beginning of eternity. He who spoke almost everything into existence now speaks to us (Matthew 4:4).

We hear Elohim (First Person of the GodHead) speaking in vs. 3, the first recorded words:

"Let there be light".

To whom was He speaking? Pause and think about it. There are definite references revealing The One speaking in the beginning, one being John 1:1-14. Check it out!

Let us pause for a moment while we observe the instant obedience of the elements in response to The Spoken Word. God speaks and it is so (Genesis 1: 1-15). The instant obedience of the elements to the Word is an implied instruction to the believer. It is one we should embrace without question. God has included the plan of obedience in order to reward our lives in this life and in the world to come. Our instant obedience to The Word of God and to His Spirit is no guarantee our journey will be easy but that it will give us the expected end that God has planned for us (Jeremiah 29:11-13), We can be sure of our future as we walk in absolute obedience.

As you become seasoned in rightly dividing The Word, you will acquire confidence in your beliefs as The Holy Spirit continually reveals Truth to your new born again spirit man. He will bear witness, with The Holy Spirit, of authenticity. After being persuaded, you will become more confident as you handle the revealed Word of God. All doubts will diminish as your appetite increases.

There are many *deep things* within the scripture, (1 Corinthians 2:10) even things not revealed in the Logos. When rightly dividing The Word we will find clarity bringing spiritual understanding to what once seemed to be mysterious. However there is a need to take caution by using temperance, (a fruit of the Spirit; Galatians 5:22-23) keeping personal curiosity at a safe level and not being lured into the hazardous wilderness of which we spoke earlier. Don't be curiously tempted to wander off into a place of private interpretation and self-nurtured carnal understanding (Proverbs 3:4-5). This could possibly give birth to undocumented 'Babel' or 'another gospel' (Galatians 1:8.). Our new spirit man, led by the Holy Spirit Guide, is trustworthy and should always remain our final authority. We must diligently stay under His protection, with our faith being able to stand against the fiery darts of the enemy. He is always ready to infiltrate and confuse our train of thought (Ephesians 6:11-18).

The Battle of the Mind,' by Joyce Myers, reveals that it is in the mind where spiritual warfare rages non-stop. At this very moment, while writing these words, I continue to stand against doubt and uncertainty of being able to accomplish the goal set before me. I continue trusting while remembering I am in God's hands and He is able to keep me through every temptation to give up and give in to my sinful defeated nature (1 Corinthians 10:13).

Try keeping your mind free and clear of distractions when handling The Word. Know The Holy Spirit Guide leads us into all Truth, while keeping the enemy at bay (John 16:13). He is our helper and He empowers us to complete the work to which God has assigned us. (Philippians 1:6).

The more we study scripture the more fortified we remain. We will inevitably experience spiritual warfare while seeking to grow stronger in our relationship with God (Ephesians. 6:6-18, Ps.149:6-6, and 1 Corinthians.10:4-6). The enemy's greatest fear is that we will become knowledgeable of our inheritance, including the power God has given His children (John 1-11).

Don't be surprised if you should suddenly become very sleepy, thirsty or hungry.

Your telephone might ring incessantly when you are in study, prayer or meditation. Long lost relatives might show up at your door in the midst of your study. Recognize it for what it is, *a distraction!*

These are times we must press in by way of fasting and prayer. Strengthen the armor of God, especially the Helmet which reminds us of what we already know to be true. Continuing to stand, we cast down vain imaginations which play tricks with our godly discipline and newfound zeal for the knowledge of God (2 Corinthians 10:3-6).

We are now in the beginning. You are there!

Genesis 1:1-25 gives an on the spot account as the Creator continues the first five days creating everything that was ever to be created. On the sixth day we are made aware *He is not alone as* He speaks once again; but this time He speaks collectively:

"Let US make man in our image, after our likeness..." (Genesis 1:26-30 AMP)

Chapter 21

How Does He Look?

Perhaps the question may arise within our finite limitations; What is the likeness and Image of the Godhead? This might very well stimulate speculation because we have no foreknowledge of the Godhead's image or likeness. One's perspective might vary according to what has been rumored, at best providing a mere imagery based on one's imagination. How does one visualize or imagine one made in the likeness and image of The Godhead whom we have not seen? We don't know what God looks like. There has been no physical photo, portrait, or drawing, not even a sketch handed down for posterity.

Will you decide according to hearsay, rumors, or popular opinion? Maybe you are impressed by what the pastor has said. Perhaps a picture on your wall or in a book from the library will help you decide.

There are a few clues as to the appearance of the Son of God. According to scripture, He was not at all attractive as some would choose to believe but uncomely, unattractive (Isaiah 53:2 KJV). He is said to be of brazen hue with wooly hair. What if The Savior of the world resembled my worst enemy? God forbid! Would I still be able to sing love songs to Him during praise and Worship? Would I be able to make my request known, or would I be too proud?

Surely, by now you must have realized, unlike Elohim, we are unable to create something from nothing, even in our wildest imagination. Anything we might imagine is composed of things already in existence. Anything ordinary would certainly be unfit for The Master's original stamp of approval.

I am reminded of a story I once heard which told of a man who boasted of himself being equal with God in his ability to create. He would prove his claim by creating his own world, choosing to begin with the creation of his man. Dramatically removing his outer jacket and rolling up his shirt sleeves, as in the flamboyant style of a magician, the young man stoops to collect dirt from the ground. God interrupts with a gentle rebuke calling to his attention that the very dirt in his hand was a part of God's original creation.

This example, though fictitious, serves to demonstrate the impossibility of anything being created without The Omniscient God who first started the process (John 15:5).

Scripture is not completely mute concerning the appearance of God, although, at times it may appear misleading. For example, in the Psalms, He is said to have feathers (Psalm 91). He is referred to in scripture as being a rock, a strong tower, a battle axe, a shepherd, and a hiding place. It is safe to say, one made in God's likeness and image would have some of the same characteristics of His creator. So the Creator, and the one made in His image, would be very much alike in many ways. We can all agree that God is an intelligent Spirit. He speaks, He sees, He is, without a doubt, creative. His witty ideas and inventions are inexhaustible! He excels in decorating abilities and color coordination exhibited throughout all nature.

Without having to make very many speculations, we can surmise that His most prized creation would be like The Godhead Himself, possessing many of His attributes. Like father like son.

Chapter 22

Adam and Eve

As we proceed into the essence of this manuscript, it is very important to pay very close attention to each line written. Never rush pass the seemingly insignificant text. It can be highly relevant though hardly detectable. Read content slowly and deliberately, not skipping anything as you might be so inclined. Examine each phrase, searching for context not written; but perhaps strongly implied.

Upon close examination, we witness this scripture (Genesis 1:27) taking on a plural form when speaking of the Initial creation of man.

As this text unfolds we observe Elohim creating not only man, but man and woman. Not *him* alone but *them, male* and *female together,* created He *them.*

Within the *context* we witness two becoming one! Scripture doesn't speak of the two as separate, but being one! God created them to function in unity from the beginning. The female was not made manifest in the natural. She was *without Form.* Eve existed in the spiritual realm as did the man creature. She was in the mind of God from the beginning, as were we all (Jeremiah 1:5). They were blessed *as one,* given dominion *together,* both having been created together in

God's likeness and in His image. Both being endowed with purpose, each waiting for their proper season.

God foreknew the woman. He made provisions for her although she was not yet visible or presently useful *(void)*. She had not been officially announced within the context of the scripture (incognito). She remained so until Genesis the second chapter.

Likewise, God knew each of us before the earth was formed. He has a plan for our lives ready to be manifested in the proper time and season (Ecclesiastes 3:1). When God begins to use you in your season, you need not make of yourself any reputation (Philippians. 2:7-9). Your gift will make room for you to step into your place and time (Proverbs 18:16).

God is the same yesterday, today, and forever. He is immutable (another of His Spiritual attributes). He never changes. In Him is no variables or shadow of turning (James: 1:17). You can depend on what He does or says. That includes the good, as well as the bad and the ugly (Deuteronomy 28).

Chapter 23

---·◆·---

It's Already Done

The Gospel of John, as well as the epistles, named for a specific city or region of origin, inform us that everything we know today, and in the days ahead was made by and for The Son of God, the second member of the GodHead, Jesus.

Scripture reveals there is nothing new under the sun (Ecclesiastes.1:9). God's timing is perfect. There is a time and a season for everything (Ecclesiastes 3:1-3).

For example, today's "so called" technological discoveries would be useless without the initial harnessing of electricity, which had to come first. Everything in its time and season.

Consider this:

Old Testament Prophets had visions of the hustle and bustle of our modern-day rush hour, but were limited in their description because they had nothing with which to compare. They could only give a description using the vernacular of their time. For example, referring to the modern day automobiles as chariots (Read Nahum 3:3-4).

Another example: God informed the prophet Jeremiah:

"Before I formed you…I knew you" (Jer.1: 5).

This should certainly answer the question of when life begins (context).

The blueprint, concerning Eve, with all her complex parts was concealed within Adam (mankind), although the woman was not yet manifested. Her time and season had not yet come. God already has a blueprint for your life as well (Jer.29: 11 -13).

Developing a close relationship with The Father, reading His Word daily, will allow you to stay abreast of every directional Word proceeding out of the mouth of God. You can know what the Spirit is saying to you concerning the plans He has for you in your season. God has already written The Book; however, we must be on the same page. The complete plan is finished, but there is a part, we as believers, are designed to fulfill in our season (Matthew 28:16-20).

Chapter 24

Get Ready, Get Ready:

As previously mentioned it has been noted by theologians and those learned who are well versed in the Hebrew tongue, that the word 'God' we see in chapter one of Genesis is in plural form. Elohim, a plural masculine noun, gives reference to the entire Godhead; God The Father, God The Son, and God The Holy Spirit. The Godhead is acknowledged as being present in the beginning. As we continue, scriptures will corroborate this conclusion (John 1: 1-14, Colossians l.1-17).

Elohim is identified in the very first verse of Genesis as it begins to unfold the process of His creative Genius. In Genesis 1:1, God, the spirit, is identified in verse two 'brooding,' (Genesis 1:2,MSG). We discern The Spirit as having a personality as well as feelings and emotions. Therefore, we must never refer to The Holy Spirit as 'IT.' but as He, Him or His. Is the Third Person of the GodHead mentioned in these first three verses?

Matthew 3:16-17, gives a distinct report of the Godhead in unified motion, the Father, Son, and Holy Spirit. Throughout the scriptures, as you diligently discern, you will witness many such occurrences.

As we thoughtfully read through Genesis 1:1-25, we share vivid details as the Creator continues creating, the first five days, everything that was ever to be created.

It is on the sixth day we were clearly made aware that He is not alone. He speaks once again, but this time He speaks collectively,

"Let us make man in our likeness…"

Enjoy the privileged, being able to witness The Mind of The Mighty Counselor Himself, (Isaiah 9:6) taking council within and of Himself. The creator speaks of His most precious creation, Adam. Mankind! Not an individual person, but Adam who is the sum total of mankind ever to occupy the Earth. Having the starter seed within himself, enabling him to duplicate himself (Genesis 1:28). Adam was not a GMO or mass production!

It is very important at this juncture to pay close attention to the scripture; line upon line.

Never rush pass the seemingly insignificant text. It can be highly relevant though hardly detectable. Read content slowly and deliberately, not skipping any as you might be so inclined to do. Examine each phrase, searching for context, not written, but perhaps strongly implied.

Chapter 25

The Joy The Lord...

Genesis 1: 29 - Genesis 2:4

As the scripture closes on the first chapter of Genesis, you will find many opportunities to rightly divide The Word as we see God giving Adam a quick recap of all He has provided. He blessed them and told them to be fruitful and multiply, filling the earth while having dominion (rulership) over all things; including the birds of the air and the fish of the sea.

Note the designated food is what the experts call in today's description, "A Plant Based Diet." Everything was to receive nourishment from the ground. Jehovah-Jireh had provided everything they would ever need for time and eternity. Although multiple things had not come to fruition, including the woman, they were all created in the beginning. He had declared everything to be good. The entire creation was perfect and beautiful. Mankind was to live happily ever after.

Psalm 19 records a thunderous celebration taking place as the heavenly host witnesses the joy of The Lord God Creator as He surveys all He had created, and declared it to be very good. Fellowship was now possible between Him and the chosen man creature whom He so loved, even before He formed him.

So, we find The Creator taking a well-deserved day of rest as the first chapter closes. He blessed The Seventh Day and Sanctified it. He set it apart as His Own.

It was to forever remain unlike any other day. He declared it to be Holy.

Feel encouraged to rightly divide as we proceed.

Chapter 26

Adam's Season

We have arrived at Genesis 2:1-6 (MSG), where we receive a brief recap of "the beginning of.."

We are informed in Genesis 2:5 that before anything grew out of the earth, not even shrub or grass, Elohim had sent no rain. Dew alone watered the face of the earth. This was another first, an underground watering system. We understand that although God made everything within the first 6 days, calling those things that were not as though they were, nothing had grown out of the earth. Not grass nor herbs. You are free to rightly divide The Word as we read through Genesis two and three, using those things that are recorded as evidence. Stay clear of speculations, suggestions, hypotheses, conjectures, and probables.

Throughout the remainder of the manuscript continue to rightly divide. Search behind the recorded Logos and allow the Holy Spirit to lead you into further Truth. Try the spirit behind your inflections and reflections to see if they line up with The Word of God.

Now is the time to use your bible concordances and other study guides. Search The Word, especially looking for reference scriptures to confirm the validity of what you find. If in doubt, confer with your pastor or teacher. If you are not satisfied with the results you find, ask the Holy Spirit to show you the Truth. Remember questions are a very healthy tool if your motive is pure.

Chapter 27

We Come to The Garden

In Genesis 2:8-16 we are given a distinct description of the Garden of Eden which Elohim created for the man creature to occupy and to care for. The verses depict the surrounding environment, including the waterways and abundant rich ore inhabiting the rich soil of the ground in that location. Was it through searching scripture that great wealth was uncovered by explorers arriving centuries later?

Did you rightly divide? Man's physical body contains all the rich ore and minerals contained within the soil in the original Garden of Eden

Looking back to Genesis 2:5, it seems everything was at a standstill, because it is written:

"There is not a man to till the ground".

Everything mankind would ever need had been created for time and eternity.

God, who made everything in six days, has apparently stopped progress because the scripture says there was no man. Think about it! (Selah)

Did this take The Creator by surprise? Was God caught unaware? Was this an oversight on God's part? Did he overlooked the man He created in His likeness and His image in chapter one? Did Elohim forget about Adam?

Remember, we said earlier His ways are not our ways and His thoughts are much higher than our finite intellect. After arriving at Genesis 2: 5, we witness the entire creation formerly spoken into existence earlier having no earthly or tangible appearance. Having made Adam in His image and His likeness, God, a spirit, without earthly substance or form, (it is safe to say) that the Man, likewise, had no form. Perhaps there is a need to revisit the statement in Genesis 1:1b, 'without form and void.'

Chapter 28

God's Perfect Plan

It might appear that God is unaware that He has created a spirit-man without form; therefore, incompatible with the physical substance of the rest of His creation. Could this seeming dilemma be a significant 'aha' moment, an opportunity to rightly divide?

It is necessary for you to know God has need of you. One designed to function within the specific purpose for which he or she is physically equipped. The truth is you are, we are, very important to the plan of God. Jesus would not have been able to give His Life as a sacrifice for the sin of the world without first becoming The Son of man.

The Son of God had to become the Son of man before entering into the physical world by way of the virgin womb. Therein we have The Christmas Story, The Birth of Jesus, born of woman, the virgin Mary, espoused to Joseph begotten of The Holy Spirit (Luke 1:30-36).

Jesus would not have been qualified to become our High Priest had He not dwelt among men (Hebrew 9:7) on earth. Fully Man and fully God, Jesus was the first human begotten without human intervention. He was the second Adam but without sin. We refer to His conception as The Immaculate Conception. The first Adam, the forerunner of Jesus and the second Adam were both born of The Holy Spirit (Genesis 1:26). The first Adam disobeyed and lost dominion, power, and authority. The Second Adam has come to restore that which was lost through His death, burial and resurrection (Matthew 28: 18). God created you, Adam, to be used as a Kingdom Citizen to fulfill a specific purpose. Through Christ, we have been given responsibility to take back the dominion we had in the beginning (Genesis 1:27).

Never let anyone tell you God doesn't need you. That is not true! His plan is designed to include mankind. He could have very well done it all without our involvement, but He chose to include us in the plan from the beginning.

Christ would have no reason to die were it not for you and I. Always remember, God included you, He included me from the beginning. Why? We may never know, except that's the way He wanted it. It was according to His good pleasure (Luke 22:15). He died that we might have eternal fellowship, Koi-no-ni-a (John 17:24, 1 John 1-3).

Chapter 29

---•◆•---

Superman

Let's recap. What do we know?

God, a spirit (John 4:4), who, in the beginning, spoke (almost) everything into existence, handled nothing which consists of earthly matter.

Adam, was made in the image and likeness of His creator, a spirit, not of the earth or composed of earthly matter.

As surely as astronauts need a space suit to venture into outer space, Adam needed an earth suit, a physical body, to be able to live on this planet called earth. Adam's season had arrived! This was a job for *superman*. No one was available, capable, or equipped to carry out the specific assignment at hand. Elohim's predestined plan, already in effect, had the answer. Jehovah-Jireh was ready and able to equip Adam for his specific purpose. He will do the same in your season.

Genesis, the second chapter is chock full of things beyond my finite comprehension. See how many you are able *to rightly divide*. Any personal commentary of what is taking place in the following verses would involve great speculations, summations, hypotheses, and conjectures.

I choose not to become entangled in the wilderness of carnal thoughts and vain imaginings; speaking of *Theophanies or Christophanies,* of which I am vaguely acquainted. I choose, rather, to remain mute concerning such things, not having any scriptural confirmation, illumination, or profound Christian experience in these areas!

In order to get a close up of God, Elohim, Jehovah-Jireh, let's zoom in on whatever capacity He chooses to manifest while providing for Himself and for His purpose, a visible man now suited in flesh.

Genesis Chapter 2:1 was vague concerning the forming of the man creature. It simply tells us that God breathed into his nostrils, and he was given form. It was at that time the man creature became a living soul.

Let's mentally slow down the process as we visualize The Godhead, a spirit, as He fashions the spirit man into a physical form. Did He temporarily manifest himself as a Theophany or Christophany as in other times as implied within the Logos? The new creation, now robed in flesh, is equipped to handle physical matter, having form and purpose; and is no longer void. This is the second mention of God making man (Genesis 1: 27). This time the man has a form.

Did you rightly divide? The only other time it is said God 'formed' is when He formed the living creatures.

Now we witness The Creator forming the man creature, thus setting the living creatures and Adam apart from all creation; which He spoke into existence by His Word alone.

Is there some significance here?

Unfortunately, this may be where unbelievers and those bordering on the edge of skepticism find cause to "abandon ship." Some may have absolute doubt as to what is recorded due to the lack of *logical* explanations. There is no immediate, on the spot confirmation. We beg for evidence given by man. We declare that "seeing is believing" and not the other way around.

On the contrary, faith declares believing is seeing (Hebrews 11:1). Throughout the scriptures we find events qualifying as illogical, unacceptable, or unbelievable, especially the Truth surrounding the Cross. There are others seen as old wives tales. For example: Daniel in the Lion's Den, The Three Hebrew Boys, Jonah and the Big Fish, The Talking Donkey, the sun standing still. These truths can only be revealed through faith.

There are occurrences in The Word we as humans are not able to explain in the natural. They have been accomplished in the supernatural or in the Spirit realm where everything has its origin. The bible declares that things seen are temporal, and things not seen are eternal. There are things we will not understand while on earth.

Some things Jesus' disciples found hard to accept, yet they followed, trusting and obeying (John 14:1-5). Many saints of old lived to see numerous things come to pass, as you will see, (John 14:12) even more extensively.

Through constant study, and steady application of The Word, you will discover, as well as discern, supernatural happenings within the pages of The Bible. The Logos will surely become Rhema, alive with the Spirit. Through the written Word you will become acquainted with believing what you once thought unbelievable or physically impossible. Now you have undeniable evidence of the supernatural being manifested in your personal life (Joshua 1:8).

Prayerfully, when you complete this book, you will have gained clear insight of the importance of laboring in the scriptures. Although we were not given much detail in Genesis 2, because of recorded reference scriptures, we are able to peer over the shoulder of God as He forms the first human from the dust of the ground, the very *first cadaver* (James 2:22).

Can you discern this prophetic act?

Molded out of the Earth by The Hands of God, Adam is filled with the precious ores, minerals, and elements found in the Garden of Eden (Genesis 2:19;3).

Although equipped with every organ, vein, muscle, tissue, and sinew, the man creature was yet lifeless. It isn't until the Living God breathes into His special creation, His own breath, does Adam become a living soul. We witness another first to be recorded in the book of beginnings; the very first mouth-to-mouth resuscitation. The Omniscient, Omnipresent, Omnipotent God breathes into the nostrils of the newly created being, His very own Spirit-Life (Zoe).

Adam immediately becomes a living, *supernatural* creature having three parts: Spirit, Soul, and Body. A new creation, now able to carry out the purpose for which he has been created.

All jurisdiction in the earth belongs to Adam. God, a Spirit, no longer has legal authority or ownership within the earth realm. God's own legal right to affect anything in the earth has been relinquished to Adam by God's own spoken decree (Genesis 1:27). Just as in the beginning, when God spoke, all the elements obeyed. Adam now has all power over all of the universe. The King of The Kingdom decreed the transfer of power complete, Elohim, being Just and True cannot break the law which is His spoken Word.

This living soul, a vessel now containing the Spirit of The Living God, created to do The Will of God, on earth as is in heaven, is in total obedience, submission, and in control.

Chapter 30

When God Speaks

We witness The Mind and Heart of our Creator as the meditation of His heart is being revealed to us in this chapter. We, as believers, know the voice of God and we hear Him and obey him. There is cause for excitement whenever the creator speaks. He has spoken many times to the prophets of old (Hebrews 1:1-3). He yet speaks to His children, and they hear His Voice and follow Him.

Do you know the sound of His Voice?

At times in scripture He is described as having a still small voice (1 Kings 19:11-13). At other times, as rivers of living water (John 7:38). Does His voice differ when He is angry, perhaps sounding like the rolling thunder? (Job) Is it at other times gentle as the falling snow?

These are just a few of my favorite things I chose to think on during Meditation. I think about things that are Lovely, True, Honest, Pure, and Virtuous. Things that bring The Master's presence closer in intimacy (Philippians 4:8).

You too can keep your mind on pleasant thoughts. They are encouraging when the enemy is trying to insight mental harassment or discomfort. Recall a few of your favorite thoughts. Give evidence that your thoughts are of Him. Count your blessings. Name them one by one.

Upon placing him in the beautiful garden. we witness Elohim giving the man creature the first commandment (Read aloud slowly, Genesis 2:16-17).

Chapter 31

———◆———

Desire of The Heart

We observe Elohim speaking another prophetic assessment, revealing His concern and compassion for the man creature's absolute joy.

"It is not good that man should be alone" (Genesis 2:18).

This verse exemplifies God's name, Jehovah-Jireh, the God who provides for us before we know we have a need. Not easily discerned, God is always working a devised yet unrevealed unspoken and unrecorded plan. To everything there is a season, a time, and a purpose.

Pay close attention.

In Genesis 2:19, Elohim involves Adam in a process. He is instructed to name all the creatures of the Kingdom, but is that the only thing God is accomplishing with this assignment? In the following verses we observe an awakening in Adam as he busies himself with his first recorded act of obedience. The process of obedience to God by naming the creatures as instructed would prove rewarding. The scripture does make us aware of Adam's coming to the awareness that among the many creatures, he finds none like himself.

During the course of his assignment there emerges a 'first' which stirs within Adam called 'an emotion' (Genesis 2:20). In hindsight, we understand Elohim quickened within man the first desire of his heart, a stirring of what was already lying dormant within the man creature. Until now, there had been no evidence of Adam having a thought of companionship.

Note:

This is an excellent opportunity to address those in authority, specifically parents.

Whatever surrounds you or your children will create desires, habits, addictions, or lifestyles resulting in future characteristics that are positive and/or negative. Everything, including eating habits, leisure, music, travel etc. will become a determining factor in the choices your loved ones make (Psalm 51:5a). There will arise desires from within according to one's exposure and the frequency and depth of that exposure. These things are molding and shaping you.

How are the desires of those for whom you are responsible being shaped?

Adam was influenced through observing the interaction among the creatures. This awakened a desire within Adam. God had created the desire from the beginning. God ignites that same desire which was lying dormant within Adam to be awakened at the proper time according to God's Perfect Will. God, in turn, fulfilled the God given desire by creating companionship for Adam.

There are desires and appetites lying dormant within us, as well as within our loved ones. Our children have desires they are not yet aware of. God has a time scheduled for each awakening. There are some desires which should not be awakened; however, because of our sin nature they are stirred by our environment and workers of iniquity.

It is up to parents and guardians to provide a wholesome atmosphere for our young people. Primarily set the proper examples. "Do what I say do and not what I do" is not working. What we behold, we become.

What have we learned from Adam's experience? God gives us the desires of our hearts according as He wills, when He wills. Adam was obedient to the Word of His Creator, diligently naming the creatures. Elohim rewarded his obedience (Psalm 37:4).

We are not informed as to how long Adam was without a help mate, or how long it took to name the creatures. We do know Adam's need was met as he is given the desire of his heart.

Awakening from sleep, not having participated in any way, Adam speaks, readily identifying the revealed new creature as, bone of his bone and flesh of his flesh (Genesis 2:23). Adam now has someone with whom he can identify.

Take note of the woman's arrival. It was on time and in her season, according to God's design and purpose before the foundation of the earth. She was not manifested a minute too soon or a second too late. She didn't have to pray for a companion. God had already prepared the woman for her debut back in Genesis 1:7.

Other 'firsts' are witnessed here, namely the scriptural edicts concerning what we presently recognize as marriage. A mind set of priorities and loyalties while introducing concepts of 'father and mother,' 'leaving and cleaving.' (Leaving what and going where?)

This is evidence of the prophetic nature of Elohim, calling those things that are not as though they already were. We just trust and obey our source (Proverbs 3: 4-5). If he said it, He will bring it to pass.

Have you ever pondered the significance of the phrase: *it came to pass*? Think about it.

There are some things recorded in Scripture we often allow to go unnoticed. For example, in The Sermon on The Mount, Jesus gives deeper insight into familiar sayings and beliefs (Matthew 5:21-48). We need to reach beyond the Logos, or the letter of The Word into the spirit realm where true life originates before it's made manifest in the natural. We will discern many potent things that give birth right before our spiritual eyes (2 Corinthians 2:9-10).

There is no record of length of days enjoyed by the couple during 'The Dispensation of Innocence,' where complete harmony, ultimate order, and peace filled the atmosphere. Adam had everything he needed. The garden was void of sin, and without distress or fear. Everything was good.

Adam chose to call his helpmate woman because she was taken out of man. He did not give her a personal name until after The Fall (Genesis 3:20). The scriptures are silent concerning the time spent in this utopian setting, perhaps days, months, years, or decades. We do not know. We are only told that it *came to pass*.

In the final chapter of this experience we will see a lot of interesting developments, many of which are firsts occurrences, giving us a great opportunity to rightly divide The Word of Truth.

Chapter 32

———◆———

Paradise Lost...

This, without a doubt, is the shortest, yet most significant chapter of this entire experience.

We, who are familiar with The Word of God, realize the dilemma which is about to face The all knowing God. We know He is about to be put into an uncompromising position. Being a just and equitable God, there is no question that He must obey as well as execute His own Decree. There are no exceptions. He must deal objectively with the eternal consequences following the first act of disobedience committed by the First Adam. Regrettably, another first described in this third and final chapter allows us to partake of what is happening behind the scenes. We get to be up close and on the set.

It seems accurate to say the Creator walks. As we learned, the man creature heard Elohim walking in the cool of the day. By reason of the inquiry by God to Adam, questions might well be raised. Let's listen.

"Adam, where are you?"

Is Elohim speaking of Adam's location alone? Surely The Omnipresent God knows Adams' whereabouts, or is there a deeper connotation?

We have reason to discern The Creator is accustomed to having Adam nearby, at least close enough to sense His presence as well as to expect him to respond. Was the Man Creature out of order? Did Elohim make a strange attempt in calling out to Adam? Was this unusual? Was it necessary for Elohim to inquire of Adam's whereabouts? Isn't God all knowing?

What would you rightly divide from this verse?

You are about to become an eyewitness to the most monumental occurrence recorded in the annals of scripture that come second only to the Death, Burial, and Resurrection of Our Savior, Jesus the Christ. This final chapter is often referred to as 'The Fall of Man.'

Characteristic of the Bible, this chapter richly avails to us the excellent opportunity to rightly divide The Word of Truth. Some opportunities are obvious, some not so obvious. Not only should you allow this exercise, to give your spirit man a work out, but be ready with pen and paper. Start a journal or a blog. You might find yourself getting an unction which awakens you out of your sleep to record what The Spirit is revealing to your spirit in the middle of the night. He never slumbers or sleeps.

If and when He leads you to a particular scripture, examine the text carefully and let the Holy Spirit help you crack some mysteries. Get excited. Share what The Spirit allows you to; otherwise keep still until He tells you to share and with whom to share it.

It is important to realize, when Adam fell, he fell from The Grace and assurance of Jehovah-Jireh's divine provision. When he fell, we all took the identical fall, and were simultaneously separated from our life source. Being in the loins of Adam, it became our equal inheritance (Romans 5:19), once again exemplifying the necessity to be BORN AGAIN.

Though none of this took our Creator by surprise, it was painful because of His Great Love for the man creature (Ephesians 2:1-3). He knew in the proper Dispensation He would have to give His life. (Can you recall in which Dispensation this Truth occurs?)

As a result of one act of disobedience we were all placed in a state of destitution without a plea. Our new lot was that which the world is partakers if today, without hope including, homicide, suicide, bullying, assassinations, molestation, human trafficking, school bombings, terrorism, starvation, and the homeless. We can go on and on into infinitum.

However, God in His rich mercy, did not abandon us (Eph. 2:4-10). He had, from the beginning, provided The Way of escape and a way back to The Father (John 14:6).

Chapter 33

————◆◆◆————

How did you do?

There are things revealed as well as things concealed. There are also things implied within the Logos. With the help of The Holy Spirit we must diligently avoid embellishing, adding to or taking away from, the documented text (Bliptures).

Try to allow your new spirit man in you to be led by The Holy Spirit into all truths, even Truths not recorded in The Logos. God has given gifts to The Body of Christ to help us uncover a portion of the supernatural and miraculous within His Word.

Further study of The Word (1Corinthians 12) will teach you of the wealth God has given His Church. More importantly He has given us precious Fruit of The Spirit; which is the power that transforms us through His Word. It has been planted in us. We are seed bearers of the Fruit of the Spirit. Without the Fruit of the Spirit The Gifts are useless. The first of The Fruit is Love (Galatians 5:22-24).

True to form, Genesis remains a book of discovery and illumination, calling to discerning eyes and ears. In the very beginning of the chapter we see significant 'first' occurrences:

    a.   Unlike any other beasts of the field, the serpent characterized (subtle) but never identified

b. We find the serpent speaking (v.1) We are able to discern from scripture context, the serpent had been observing as well as listening, and had knowledge of what God said (v1).
c. Woman distorts (The Word) what God said (v.3)
d. The first lie as well as the first liar (v.4)
e. he first deception (v.5)
f. The first temptation (v.6)
g. The first act of covetousness (v.6)
h. The first act of insubordination(v.6)
i. The first emotion of Shame (v.7)
j. The first act of fear (v.10
k. The first domestic disturbance (v.12)
l. The first blame game (v.12-13)

There are other 'firsts' One of the most significant 'first' occurrences is the prophetic declaration concerning the Spiritual Warfare.

The most ancient war ever declared and will continue until God says it's over (Revelations 20:16).

Did you discern…

a. In which verses was spiritual warfare prophesied?
b. Agape love displayed in God's ejection of fallen man.
c. Act of Elohim's love, mercy, and Justice.
d. What did you discern in the recording of Jesus referring to himself as Alpha and Omega?'
e. What do you discern from the prophecy coming from God which spoke of the serpent having to crawl on his belly?
f. What was significant concerning the sewing of fig leaves?
g. How did the human creatures 'SEE' before their eyes were open?

Epilogue

Elohim, having foreknowledge, knowing the end from the beginning, had recorded everything, including cause, effect, and remedy within His predestined plan before the foundation of the world.

He truly does have the whole world in His Hand.

I implore you. Get a Rottweiler grip onto the contents of this book along with context. Seek other dividers of The Word who will lift your arms of faith as you press for higher plains. Continue to learn, applying what you learn daily. Become doers of the word. Those things which are unclear, store away and pray for clarity. Never let go of what is scripturally sound. You will receive what God has in store for those who truly love Him.

Stay open to The Holy Spirit's correction. Don't place God in a box.

Take the limits off. In so doing, you allow Him to reveal even things not revealed in the Logos.

I am reminded of the scripture which states:

"Well done my good and faithful servant. You have been faithful over a few things. I will make you ruler over many." I believe this scripture speaks of worlds and assignments to come. It appears to me that the completed work down here is preparing us to rule and to reign in the world(s) to come. There is a great cloud of witnesses cheering us on to the finish line.

Forerunners such as Abraham, Noah, Moses, Joshua, David, Elijah, Paul, and Peter to name a few, through their love affair with Our Creator, Enjoyed, with anticipated excitement, many secrets involving the plan and The Will of God. When you are faithful, you will exceed the exploits of those gone before you.

God will trust you with His secret things through discernment, illumination, and revelations (2 Corinthians 2:9).

The following are scriptures you may want to research and even memorize.

May they encourage, challenge, and strengthen you.

Continue growing in Grace in your diligent pursuit of the knowledge of our Lord and Savior.

Matthew. 6:33, John 11:26, John 14:18-23, Romans 1:17-18, 8:28,12, 1-3, Romans 8:1, 1 Corinthians. 10:5, 4-8, 15:58, 2 Corinthians 2:17-20, Galatians 5:1, 6:9, Ephesians 6:11-18, 1 John 1:9, 3:1-3, 4: 7-8, 3 John 2, Philippians 4:4-19, Hebrews 13:5 (Deuteronomy 31:6)

The Lord has need of workers. The fields are ripe unto harvest, but the laborers are few and many are confused. Pray to the Lord of The Harvest, that He may send more laborers to work in the field (the world).

May you be motivated to serve. Souls are dying for lack of knowledge.

There is so much work to be done.

The Lord willing, following sequels, as well as an upcoming website, a blog and more will become available for a deeper fellowship.

Desire the Sincere Milk that you may grow thereby.

Contact information:
Marge Stewart
motherdancer@outlook.com
motherdancer02@gmail.com
Greensboro N.C.
631 316 6035

Inquiring minds want to know, what Does The Word Say?

Can you lose your salvation?

What is the Baptism of The Holy Spirit?

Can you be saved without The Holy Spirit?

How many Baptisms are there?

Do you have to be Baptized to be saved?

What does it mean to be saved?

Where is the presence of God?

Can you bury a spirit?

Were there any appearances of Jesus in the old testament?

With Whom did Jacob wrestled all night?

What is The Rapture?

Are the Rapture and The Second Coming the same?

Will we see Jesus when He comes in The Rapture?

Acknowledges: The issue of my heart is Gratefulness

I acknowledge my Lord and Savior Jesus, The Christ, who lives in me and in whom I live, move, and have my being. Without Him and His Holy Spirit, I could do nothing.

I praise The Holy Spirit for gently constraining me with His temperance and gentle admonishments through the process. He is indeed the wind beneath my wings.

Dedicated to my two beloved pastors:

Pastor Emeritus: Albert L. Brown, Riverhead, N.Y.
Pastor Michael Thomas, Greensboro, N.C./Kernersville, N.C.

Printed in the United States
By Bookmasters